Inner Thoughts

Derrick L Boone

BluSapphire Books
(Revised Edition)

© 2013 Derrick L Boone. All rights reserved.

No part of this book may be reproduced, stored in a retrieval system, or transmitted by any means without the written permission of the author.

Published by Blu Sapphire LLC 3/4/2013

ISBN: 978-0-6922-2410-6

Any people depicted in stock imagery provided by Thinkstock are models, and such images are being used for illustrative purposes only.
Certain stock imagery © Thinkstock.

Table of Contents

Thoughts 1 – *Desire*   4

In My Sleep	5
Another Day Of Loneliness	6
Divine	7
First Sight	8
You Are The One	9
Magical Love	10
All Times	11
Desire Holds No Boundary	12
Are We Dreaming	13
Those Words	14
You	15
Everyday	16
At Ease	17
Daydream	18
Precious	19
Lesson Of The Heart	20
Emotional Love	21
Curiosity	22

Thoughts 2 – *Hurt*   23

Untitled	24
What You See	25
The One You Love (Who Don't Love You)	26
The Pain Inside	27
Untitled2	28
Understand	29

Thoughts 3 – *Thought*   30

How Come	31
Thoughts	32
I Told You	33
Just Thinking	34
Secret Mind	35

Thoughts 4 – *Hope*   36

At Teardrop Mountain	37
Water Stand Still For Me	38
Patience	39
Stormy Days	40
Winter In Spring	41
Don't Run	42
Natural Love	43
This Is A Pressure World	44
Situation Is Not Right	45
Confusion	46
We Need Adjustment (In This Time)	47
What Is This	48
Feel Of Soul	49
How Funky Can We Get	50
So On	51
Magic Cloud	52

Thoughts 1

Desire:

(PSALM 34:12) Who is the man who desires life.

(Dictionary) To wish or long for.

In My Sleep

A vision so pure with elegance to the touch.
My beauty was standing, in the midst of everlasting love.
I watched her as she moved so angelically.
I called out her name, she answered with just a whisper, "Yes, my love."

A sound so angelical, I was stunned just to exhale my next thought.
I asked her, "Where is love?" She answered, "Love is where you seek it, in me." As she moved closer to hold me, her touch and body just vanished in me like we were one.

I felt peace as my soul relinquished the power of love.
My angelical beauty, no words could ever explain her essence.
Her grace can purify the hardest heart into love.
As I reached for her, her image was just a vision in my sleep.

Another Day Of Loneliness

When I look out the window to a day of darkness, I feel no embrace from behind to comfort the emptiness from within. Lord I pray, where is my divine mate? Is it the angel you sent to watch over me? Love came and vanished just like the mist on this dark day. Is it just that I teach an aching heart, but my heart is still empty... because loneliness is still here.

Still looking out the window and remembering all that has come into my life and left, wondering what the purpose of the experience was. Because I'm still lonely with nobody beside me. The tears I cry, is the love I want, but when they fall, it has no substance for my love to appear in a natural form. Until then, another day of loneliness.

Divine

It doesn't exist in the presence of my life. The unknown always has me grasping for faith. Stillness holds my soul together, as heaven holds love. Oh heaven you ask, why is love running from me? Love seems to come and go like it has no existence. Loneliness appears again, in the shadow of your soul. Your soul knows there is somebody out there for you, but do you know. One day, I was told always watch what you pray for. Because anybody can be your soul mate. Your father, mother, sister, brother or friend. But what you fail to ask is for the person to exist when you exist. Your Divine Mate.

First Sight

When I first saw you, all I wanted to tell you was how beautiful you were. My mind was talking those words, but my mouth spoke emptiness. Shyness overcame me just as light overcomes darkness.
I'm reaching out to you, but my presence is like a ghost to you because you don't know that I exist.
Everyday you walk by.
The same time, I watch you as though you are coming to see me.
That's when I fell in love at first sight.
I never thought I would fall for a woman just by sight.
BUT I DID!

You Are The One

Like on a cloudy day when the sun peeps through the clouds and shines it's rays on down. That's the way I felt when I saw you. You brighten up every lost hope in my heart. The way you talk, I'm hanging on every word. Everything about you is so God-like. It feels like you are the Garden of Eden in the flesh.

Your presence specifies beauty. I guess what I'm trying to say is that you are the one. When I prayed for that divine lover, here you are. Right in the mist of my reach. I'm so motionless - like you froze time. It felt like eternity within those few minutes. Being around beauty and wisdom wrapped up in one soul. I'm fortunate to be around somebody like you. I guess what I'm trying to say is that you are the one - until I find the nerve to speak.

Magical Love

I appear in your mind with spiritual and physical love.
Just an image of your imagination.
Just like a magic show when a ribbon is torn into pieces.
Like a dove, I will appear with your type of love.

All Times

I know hurt is a hard thing to overcome. When trust is hard to find, I will be there all times. Moments you search and wonder what it's going to take. But it won't take much with me, baby. As I look into your eyes, I see love all times. I feel the pain of love; just like you do. To overcome that, open your heart and I will open mine. Love is a wonderful place to dwell, all times.

Desire Holds No Boundary

As the sunsets, nighttime falls on the city like when a lover covers his beauty, after making unexplainable love. When thinking about his love while driving down the city streets. Each time he passes the city lights, it feels like his beauty's heartbeat, when the passion is intense. The shadows of the night remind him of their silhouette in the bedroom when both of them are making love in darkness. As the candlelight cast shadows of their souls. The sky holds the moon, like when he holds his beauty and whispers in her ear.

My desire holds no boundary for your love.

When driving in the city of love, he feels the air blow through his window, as it kisses his face. He tries to caress it, as he thinks about that brown skin beauty's touch. The night brings a mystical feel as he drives in the city of love. Looking at the stars seems like every spot he kisses on his beauty's body. They point the way to ecstasy. He absorbs all the city's energy in his soul. The abyss of joy enters his heart when he finally makes his destination.

Desire Holds No Boundary for your love (He Whispers).

Are We Dreaming

Are we dreaming baby, because everything is going right. The way we handle this love thing is amazing. It's like the sun and moon always working together. The way they show support for each other is like our love, baby.

Are we dreaming baby? When I hold your hand, ecstasy races through my body. In a world where nothing but love exist. As we make love it feels like two spirits floating across the dense universe. In our world, love is everlasting. As we lay here together holding each other tight. My love is drained from your soft brown body.

As we dream, this is truly a love thing, baby. Relax. Free your mind from the reality of the world and I will free my mind from the worries of the world. In our world, love is everlasting. So let's float together across the heavens. Baby we are one, because this love is so unique.

Those Words

It's like being there for the very first time when those words were given existence.

My soul felt the meaning, as those words were given meaning.
Your lips spoke those words in a spirit form.
It felt like GOD had cleansed my soul.
A feeling that does not have a description.

I can see things other people can't see.
I can feel things other people can't feel.
Your lips spoke this feeling.
Your lips spoke, as if those words had sexuality.

I'm lost in the presence of your being.
My breath has inhaled those words and my heart exhaled loneliness
I feel blessed because those words that have been uttered into existence are!

I Love You

You

Since the day of time, I cannot explain the mystery that surrounds you. All I know is that heaven above has descended on me because of you. You are like the Alpha and Omega of love. Things I could not explain, I now understand their every existence. If this world was meant to be conquered, then I will conquer it because of you. Just touch me baby. Let me feel like a baby being caressed by it's mother. You make my pain and suffering in this world vanish with just a kiss. All of this I feel, because of you being you. I'll be loving you forevermore. (YOU)

Everyday

As I think about the love I have, I look out the window and watch the rain.
As my lady holds me, I forget about the pain.
It's not a day I don't want her by my side.
She fills my heart with love, as I sit back and reside.

Every day I think about her body and soul.
Every day I just want her to hold.

The presence of her aura captivates me like a beam of light.
I'm always trying to find quality time for the two of us.

Every day and Every night.
Sure goodness comes from her smile as it purifies my day like a little child.
All I do is think about her.
I ask myself is there something wrong with me.
I guess not, it's just love you see.

Every day I think about her body and soul.
Every day I just want her to hold me.

As I think about the love I have.
I look out the window and the sun is out.
Knowing I know what the days are all about.

Derrick L Boone

At Ease

It's a joy to have a woman like you. A mind so intelligent.
Skin as soft as silk. As I sing to you, be at ease. Relax and
cruise with the quiet storm. You are my gift. You deserve the highest
respect. We might have our ups and
downs, but baby our faith will overcome.

As I look into your eyes, tears fall from mine, because I see
what you went through.

Baby, pain is a terrible thing to experience. The struggles
it can take you through. I will be at your side as we journey the
path of life. So forgetful, that you can forgive somebody
of their wrong doing. So just rest baby and be at ease. So
beautiful like a queen.

As I look into your eyes, tears fall from mine because I see
what you went through.

Here, baby, sip this wine. Love is in the air. Just let me sing
to you, baby. Let me make you feel at ease. Beautiful as
the moonlight's glimpse off your pretty brown eyes. A smile
so cheerful, it will uplift a heart. To show the world you are
not down. So baby, close your eyes and fall in a magical dream.
Just be at ease.

Daydream

Hey, lovely lady. I see you worrying about love.
Come with me and lets talk about making you
alright about love. Lady, look into my eyes.
Look deep. My love for you is everlasting.
Don't worry about unfaithfulness; that's
not going to happen. So hold on baby, let's
daydream together.

Way up in the sky, daydream as high.
That's how our love is going to fly.

You're an intelligent black lady looking for a
love that's true and I'm going to try my best
to fulfill that. I was brought up to respect my
African queens. So, baby, let's make this thing
happen. As I look into your eyes, you seem
sincere and inquisitive about love. It will work as
long as we have faith in each other.

Way up in the sky, daydream as high.
That's how our love is going to fly.

Precious

Precious are the days within you when the loving is right.
I know that your heart is fulfilled tonight.
I'm just sitting back thinking about love.
How to make you feel better every day and make the joy stay.

It's like watching a child play so happy inside. Sometimes
you want to cry because you know that child has peace inside it's heart.
So, baby, as I think about love, you will be satisfied like an angel within
your soul. Because I'm there manifesting your heart.

Lesson Of The Heart

Caress me if you dare, because you know the attraction is there.
Like a dove that symbolizes the freedom we have.
As the birds gracefully glide across the sky, that's how our hearts feel you and I.

Your boldness, caresses me as we fell in an emotional bliss.
Sunken in a world all ours, feeling each other's souls.
We don't know if this is meant to be. All we know is that this is a lesson of the heart.

Ecstasy controls us, as we don't want the feeling to depart as we study the unknown in each other's heart.

Emotional Love

It's a tricky situation when I'm thinking of you.
My feelings revolve around you.
When the both of us kiss, it's like a magical universe that surrounds us.
Two people should carry a bond that is everlasting.

Oh, yeah, baby, when I touch you, your body just vanishes as if we are one. As our hearts race back and forth with a feeling that you can't explain. Just think about the pleasure we are now sharing.
In this emotional love when your mind is playing an emotional game.

Curiosity

The first time I saw you, curiosity entered my mind. As the days prolonged and we spent time together, all I thought about was how it would be. We made mental foreplay when we were together. Trying to capture any glimpse of body language; to let each other know when the time was right. As night fell, the presence of your soul covered me like a blanket.

All I have is this curiosity. I have somebody in my life and you do too. But human nature is taking control of our inner selves. Is this supposed to happen like this? I waited for a sign and curiosity was there, manifesting within my soul, as if I was caught up in the rapture. I know this love affair is going to happen - just one time to see how you are. This is tearing my soul apart. That night you called me to come over and the mood was right. The curiosity came non-stop.

The next day we knew we would never be the same. But still we went our separate ways. That's curiosity for you, revealing that the grass is not always greener on the other side.

Thoughts 2

Hurt:

(Dictionary) To cause mental pain.

Untitled

Oh, when we met it was so magical.
I thought love was never like this.
You were like an angel that had descended from heaven.
So pure and innocent I never met a person like you before.

The times we spent together.
My heart was growing as though you were a teacher.
Teaching it a lesson in love.

As the angel in you spread over me like a spiritual being.
I felt love for the first time.
Oh, how wonderful it is to feel joy in myself again.

But what it all came out to be is that.
Was love really love?
So is this what relationship are all about?
Happiness to sadness.

Derrick L Boone

What You See

The first time you laid your eyes on me,
you said you fell in love with me.
Then the times you spent with me,
you said you loved my ways and my personality.

Everything about me is what you were looking for in a man.
You told me I was the one.
Deception blinded me only if I knew your agenda…
Was different from your point of view.

Now you are trying to make me out to be somebody I'm not.
Thinking to mold my mind like clay.
By using psychology for me to change.
Downgrading everything about me, while at first you said you loved me and everything about me.

So now you think I'm your project to tame
Girl, you must think I'm a damn fool.

The One You Love (Who Don't Love You)

All I want is to make things right.
I try to share my love but all you do is put up a fight,
not to open your heart for me tonight.
As I struggle to see what went wrong,
I can't see an answer to my lonely song.

Life itself.

As the one you try to love don't respect love.
I put out my heart to you.
You seem cold like I don't love you.
It hurts like hell to try to love somebody who does not love you.
GOD tells me to be strong because he said, he will always love me.

The Pain Inside

The hurt inside is so embedded.
Tears can't escape my soul.
You told me that you wouldn't waste my time when it came to love.
But what you told me became a lie.
You made love seem harder than it really was.

So now I sit here coping with the pain inside.
Trying to understand
when you told me that I was less than a man.

When you told me that I respect you.
That I'm the perfect gentleman for you.
But your heart condemns you to love me.
I'm so confused, while my emotions are ripping me apart.
I don't understand you and I guess I never will.

So I sit here coping with the pain inside.
Sometime I feel like I want to leave and sometimes I don't.
But my heart is telling me to.

There's a war going on in my soul.
Finding a way to cope and understand.
So I guess I have to end it and face,
THE PAIN INSIDE

Untitled 2

Why doesn't love stand the test of time?
It's hard to find two hearts that are intertwining with the mind.
Mistaking love for a business and not for what's within. Heaven knows that the way things are going on is not right.

When two people are not serious about the aspect of life and take the heart for granted.
Their relationship is just idling.
As if love is just a word.
They are not feeling love from within.

As words with no meaning filter
out their mouth - as if they care about each other.
Heaven knows that
the way things are going on is not right.
How can you act on love and not feel
Love?
I guess that's just human nature! My love.

Understand

Baby, I understand the problems in the past.
I understand the bad relationships you had.
I know your heart is cold toward men,
I understand your heart can mend.
Let's talk and communicate together.
Because I understand the stormy weather.
Don't think you are the only one in the world that's been hurt.

Yes, I understand.

Yes, I'm a man who feels too.
So I have been hurt just like you.
So I understand the pain you went through.
Everyone has some trials and tribulations in their life.
Just talk to me tonight.

Yes, I understand.

Open your heart, let me wander in.
So I can be that special kind of friend.

Yes, I understand.

I understand all that you went through.
Because you love me and I love you.

Yes, I Understand.

Thoughts 3

Thought:

(PSALM 94:11) The LORD know the thoughts of man, That they are futile.

(Dictionary) The product of mental activity.

How Come

How come snow falls in the wintertime and not in the spring?
How come lovers always have different dreams?
When their hearts are different in between.
Trying to figure a way to bring their hearts together for love to stay.
How come it's hard to keep love together these days?

Thoughts

How many times do you sit down and think about
the good times and the bad?
I tell you, it's a crazy thing.

On one lonely night, you sit there alone
thinking about the good times you been through.
It seems like you were on top of the world.

Then here comes the bad times.
To make you as low as if you can't take any more.
You all know what I'm talking about,
everybody has had those thoughts.

As time moves on, you think about the things in the past
that won't happen in your life any more.
Because of the hurt you have to endure.
As the future came across your mind.
The thoughts of staying strong always conquers
the hurt and pain of the past.

I Told You

Somebody told me, they were in love and that person loves them too.

But speculation had that person thinking that love can't come true.
I told them that love is there waiting for you.
Past relationships clouded the mind, they just thought about the negatives at that time.

They told me this person is there for them through the thick and thin but their mind still couldn't comprehend.
I told them this person is here for a reason, so your heart can be rebuilt for all the seasons.
You need this you see. Spring brings the joy in human beings.
Summer is the season for fun and unity.
Fall is when reality hits and winter is to show that your heart is ready for harsh times.

That's why this person is in your life, so you won't have a relationship that is hard to find.
They are there for all times.

Just Thinking

Back and forth as my mind gets caught up in a state.
Situation coming and going as an illusion in my mind.
Trying to stay afloat of this worldly bind. All I can do is meditate to find time.

Why do we trip on things we don't have control of some of the time?

Feeling overwhelmed, don't know where they're coming from.
You ask for the answer and there's no answer for them. I guess time is the only answer for this thing.

Just wishing the LORD has something to bring.
All you know is that this is a situation for you to learn from.
Time will tell the story of life.

What you wish for will be revealing.
Then you know that the lord was there to hear.
This is part of life, a play in itself and the stage we have been dealt.
Which script we get, we don't know, all we can do is go with the flow.

Secret Mind

People just don't know what goes on in my mind.
Talking about things they don't know what's going on.
The only person who knows is GOD himself.
So keep out of my business and attend to your's.

Only GOD and I know about the secret mind.
So stop wasting your time.

If I want people to know, I would do so.
So don't judge and guess, leave it alone. I think
It's the best. Secret mind for some to know.
I might be silence, but that don't mean I'm not
thinking of what's going on.

Only GOD knows what I'm thinking and saying.
Secret mind strictly your's.

Thoughts rain down but words say silent.
Only you and GOD know about the secret mind.
Your business is your's, not the whole world to know.
So stay calm because nobody knows what's in your secret mind.
So ignore the talker and live your life.

Thoughts 4

Hope:

(ROM 5:5) Now hope does not disappoint, Because the love of GOD has been poured out in our hearts by the Holy Spirit who was given to us.

(Dictionary) A particular instance of this feeling.

At Teardrop Mountain

Gazing at the pond wondering what's going to happen in the world next. A feeling of ease controls my body. Because I let go of the pain at teardrop mountain.

How wonderful it is to sit in silence and think positive about life. As I look up at the blue sky, I think to the LORD. You can cry at the mountain to let go of the sorrow, you can smile just because you are there. Alone with the moon staring as if you were a bird who could fly right to it.

The LORD knows what you're thinking. Friendly sounds surround you, because you know that the world is far behind. You can find a teardrop castle where people's tears have fallen. A site that's more beautiful than anything you have ever seen. A place for pain and to rejoice with a smile. This is a place for forgiveness and faith so you can face the world again.

"At Teardrop Mountain".

Water Stand Still For Me

Can you stand still for me, so I can follow your flow?
I would like to know where you come from and where you are going.
I see the moonlight glow off of you.
I see the blue sky reflect on you.
But I don't see myself.

So water stand still for me.
So I can see myself with you.
You are the element that is essential to life.
You are a part of me, sometimes you are calm, but you still flow.
Sometimes you are rough, but you still flow.

You are like the foundation of life.
Everything you do is like life itself.
You never flow the same.
There is always something different about you.

So water stand still for me.
So I can put life on hold, so I can follow your flow.
How deep does your water go?
Is it as deep as the pain in my soul?

If only I could be like you, when you flow to your destiny.
So I ask you…
Water can you stand still for me.
So I can find my destiny?

Patience

How important are the days, when you are waiting for the unexpected? Seeking and searching. Trying to capture time, to hold it in the midst of your life.

The days, hours, minutes and seconds are like a distant star - you see it, but just can't reach it.

Holding on to memories that have fallen in the dark corners of your soul. Trying to figure out your place on earth.
Your heart is filled with invisible tears.

As time keeps on slipping from your hold, but with patience your distance star will come to you.

Stormy Days

All I dream about is to be comfortable in life.
My destiny hasn't awakened yet.
As I stare out of the window, I see nothing but the gray clouds that
represent the times I been through in my life.
The rain constantly falls, as the tears fall from my eyes.
That you don't see, but they are there.
Hoping that the winds will guide me there, to my destiny.

Stormy days will come, but I still have faith to overcome.
Listen and you will hear the rain tell you of your life.

Stormy days let you ease your mind. Put on some soft calm music.
Just reminisce about yesterday and look forward to the days ahead.
Just like the storm when it gracefully flies by. It's just like life,
floating by waiting for something to happen.
In this weather, keep your head above those clouds and look forward.
Oh! Those stormy days are a conclusion in itself.

Derrick L Boone

Winter In Spring

This portrait is so captivating. The snow compliments the flower in it's vivid of colors. The flower is chilly due to the hint of snow surrounding it. The sun warms it like a lover's touch. The air is crisp like a kiss. Everything is in its proper place.

The snow shows purity and perfection. Winter is the start of rejuvenating. Beauty is the flower that is grace. Spring is the beginning of growth.

It's like life trying to find balance within the season. Always rejuvenating when there is growth. It warms when there is a chill. Winter breathes fresh air into spring, when the two seasons start to intertwine. Spring inhale to start the process of new life. As the sun embrace the two seasons to warm their souls. Captivating is this portrait showing the essence of life.

Don't Run

Things seem to be revolving around day by day. The closer I get to you the further you depart from me. All I want is to show you love.

GOD knows my heart has been aching for you to enter in. Why are there always complications in your life? The pressure of life is bearable when you have two people to conquer it.

I know relationships seem complicated, but when you have the LORD in your life all things are possible. Don't keep running from love. Because when you are ready for love, love will run from you.

Natural Love

Taking our time to get to know each other better.
The process of love is everlasting.
We are doing things to qualify for this test.
As I massage your mind with honesty and trust.

You prove your chivalry and loyalty to me.
As we bond in this relationship, we talk about the nature between you and me.
Problems will happen, but we are strong to conquer life's situation.
Love is a mystery in itself.
Don't be scared, it's just natural love.

This Is A Pressure World

As time flies by, problems will follow.
The pressure of the world is hard to solve.
When money is a problem can't afford to keep you alive.
Your worries last forever.
Just have faith.

Sometimes it's hard to do.
But it's just the pressure of the world.
Sorrow is a clue, what should we do.
Just have faith we'll make it through.

Seeing homeless people, it stays heavy in my heart.
As tears try to fall it's tearing me apart.
I wish there was a way for me to help.
I'm struggling to; if I keep trying I will someday be able to help too.
If there was peace across the land. This would be call heaven.
But so far it's just a dream.

Little kids are under pressure to do well.
But some are pressured to do bad things.
A positive place is where they should be.
But some are training, to hate, to lie, to steal and to kill.

This is a pressure world.
As I dream on I will always thank the LORD.
For what he has blessed me with.
The people of the world should try to do the same.

Situation Is Not Right

As a person thinks of the problems they go through,
it's seems like an everlasting road.
Worrying what's going to happen next.
I just don't understand the maze of life.
Pressure coming from every direction.
Everything you do right seems wrong.
Trying to live positive, but it turns out to be negative.
Is this life about pressure and trials?
To overcome it, it takes a strong person.

Pressure day and night, situation is not right.
The mind triggers a fight and keep your head up. It's going to be alright.

Self-esteem is low, but the heart said "No! "
People laugh as you stumble; confidence level is about to crumble.
Bring you down as low as you can go.
Saying things you can't do, but they don't know what you are going through.
Trying to make your dreams come true.
It's tough but they don't know that I'm going to fulfill my goals.

Pressure day and night, situation is not right.
The mind triggers a fight and keep your head up. It's going to be alright.

Confusion

Confused about the ways of mankind. The hate that's in the hearts
of men.
I will never feel like that. My heart is as soft as the clouds in the sky.
The environment is a substance used for beauty, not used for destruction.
Oh, man. GOD forbids this, but man doesn't care what
GOD forbids. What's happening?

Confusion in a world that was made by GOD, not man. Man can't
Understand that the world is not his.

GOD is peace and love in my eyesight. But to others, GOD is just
another myth.
We have to free the brothers and sisters whose minds are lost in hate. I
know it's hard in this world, but faith is the key. Keep working for a
better life.

Confusion in a world that was made by GOD, not man. Man can't
understand that the world is not his.

Drugs are the work of the devil.
People, listen to the right teacher, GOD. War is not right. It's painful
living for a poor child to see inflation.
High taxes, lack education, low income and no love. [That's War] world
stand still, let man stop, evaluate the problems that are happening.
The mind is matter that has a mass, but the object is to think of positive tasks.
Third eye sees to a galaxy that man can't touch, roam, destroy or build.
It's a feeling.

With a positive touch love from the heaven above that won't keep still.
Unity.

A structure of race holding hands to a different bass.

We Need Adjustment (In This Time)

As I see things in the world.
I wonder is the world a stage and we are in this play.
The feeling I have is depressing.
People not trying to suggest a better way.
As I look in the sky, there's somebody I love and that is GOD.

We need adjustment (in this time).
Feelings are strong I wonder why.
Maybe GOD is talking to me from inside.

I pray that one day crime would stop.
We need unity for this type to drop.
The sun brings joy to someone's eyes.
We need knowledge to refresh our minds.
Learn about life is the key.
Trust in GOD, he will carry you as far as you need.

We need adjustment (in this time).
Feelings are strong. I wonder why.
Maybe GOD is talking to me from inside.

Passion of love surrounds me.
When I carry out his deeds, that a child can grow up with an eye that sees the future.
GOD is LOVE.
LOVE is GOD.
One day we will be free from all the pain, that's in the world.
I would like to be a teacher in music to the people.

We need adjustment (in this time).
Feelings are strong, I wonder why.
Maybe GOD talking to me from inside.

We need love and peace.
We need knowledge.
Unity, Poetry.

What Is This

What is this, I'm getting pissed.
Life problems just don't miss.
When I wake up, I thank GOD for another day.
Then I say, "Hey:

I know the devil is on his way."
To get through this day, I have to have faith.
Oh LORD, what is it going to take for me to succeed
in a world of make believe?

What is this, I'm getting pissed. Life problems just don't miss.
When I'm trying to get myself together, something worse pops up.
Not for the better.

But I'm going to strive to stay alive.
Because I know that
GOD is by my side.

Feel Of Soul

Life, a pain in itself.
Confused about the ways of mankind.
Why does it have to be this way?
I think it's just a test for faith.
People strive for lust of power, that's why the world is going down.

As the groove set me free, funky sounds control my body.
In order to feel release, the feel of soul is in me.
If the world can feel like that, then misuse don't have to be like that.

Witness the struggle in the world as tears fall from a child
eyes. Wondering if the future is going to be like this in their lives.
Confusion has a hold, as poverty still takes control.
The message is clear. So strive for a better life.

How Funky Can We Get

As the black race struggles, there still is a little bit of unity.
Some of the rap generation is trying to bring back the black unity.
As we progress, some are still lost in a state of no morals.
We can get as funky as we want to get if we just put our minds to it.

If we keep killing our brothers and sisters what's going to happen next?
The black race might fall, but I don't think so.
Because we still have a lot of positive brothers and sisters in the world.
Black people raise their fists and stop the nonsense.

So On

I always look toward to the future and have faith of what the future's going to bring.
Some love and happiness in this magical reality.
It's hard to keep it up there as long as I live.

So on goes life, a pothole in the road. Troubles there and the next day it's gone.

So on and on that the way it goes.
Problems it seems like the whole world is under some kind of hate stage.

I don't think anything is going to get solved as long as we have people doing evil things.
In DC, a war zone like Berlin. I've never seen brothers killing like that.

So on life goes and nothing is getting better.

So on and on that's the way it goes.

Magic Cloud

As the storm pass by, there's
a wonder in my mind. A magic
cloud. Feel the heart when two
people make one, there's a feel of
unity. Problems of the world don't exists.

In the sky above all things there's a magic
cloud for all to see. A wonder in itself. The
cloud rich with rainbow colors in a world.
Where the sky is as blue as blue can get.
Floating across the dense universe. The
spirits of the unknown, happy with joy
and peace.

Magic cloud eases the smile. Magic cloud
make you feel proud. The wind blows as the
sweet smell of spring feels the air. My mind
still in a daze as I dream on. The magic cloud,
a place of reality in a dream. In the sky above
all things there are a magic cloud for all to see.
A wonder in itself. Magic cloud, some will be
there in a harmless state of mind. Freedom is the
key. Magic cloud is a place to be.

Derrick L Boone

Inner Thoughts

www.ingramcontent.com/pod-product-compliance
Lightning Source LLC
Chambersburg PA
CBHW061515040426
42450CB00008B/1633